The Essential
George Gershwin
Piano Solos

Exclusive Distributors:
Music Sales Limited
8/9 Frith Street, London
W1V 5TZ, England.

Music Sales Pty Limited
120 Rothschild Avenue, Rosebery,
NSW 2018, Australia.

Order No. AM964030
ISBN 0-7119-8174-4
This book © Copyright 1988, 2000
by Wise Publications

Unauthorised reproduction of any
part of this publication by any means including
photocopying is an infringement of copyright.

Compiled and arranged by Frank Booth
Cover design by Paula Snell Design
Photographs courtesy of Hulton Getty
& Mary Evans Picture Library

Your Guarantee of Quality
As publishers, we strive to produce every book
to the highest commercial standards. This book has
been carefully designed to minimise awkward page
turns and to make playing from it a real pleasure.
Particular care has been given to specifying acid-free,
neutral-sized paper made from pulps which have
not been elemental chlorine bleached. This pulp is
from farmed sustainable forests and was produced
with special regard for the environment. Throughout,
the printing and binding have been planned to
ensure a sturdy, attractive publication which should
give years of enjoyment. If your copy fails to meet
our high standards, please inform us and we will
gladly replace it.

Music Sales' complete catalogue describes
thousands of titles and is available in full colour
sections by subject, direct from Music Sales Limited.
Please state your areas of interest and send a
cheque/postal order for £1.50 for postage to:
Music Sales Limited, Newmarket Road,
Bury St. Edmunds, Suffolk IP33 3YB.

www.musicsales.com

This publication is not authorised for sale in the
United States of America and/or Canada.

Wise Publications
London / New York / Paris / Sydney / Copenhagen / Madrid / Tokyo

An American In Paris 52

But Not For Me 41

Embraceable You 19

Fascinating Rhythm 44

A Foggy Day 22

I Got Rhythm 60

It Ain't Necessarily So 8

Oh, Lady, Be Good 47

The Man I Love 25

Nice Work If You Can Get It 5

Rhapsody In Blue 2

Somebody Loves Me 36

Strike Up The Band 28

Summertime 11

They Can't Take That Away From Me 33

'S Wonderful 14

Rhapsody In Blue

By George Gershwin

Arrangement based on the orchestration by Ferde Grofe

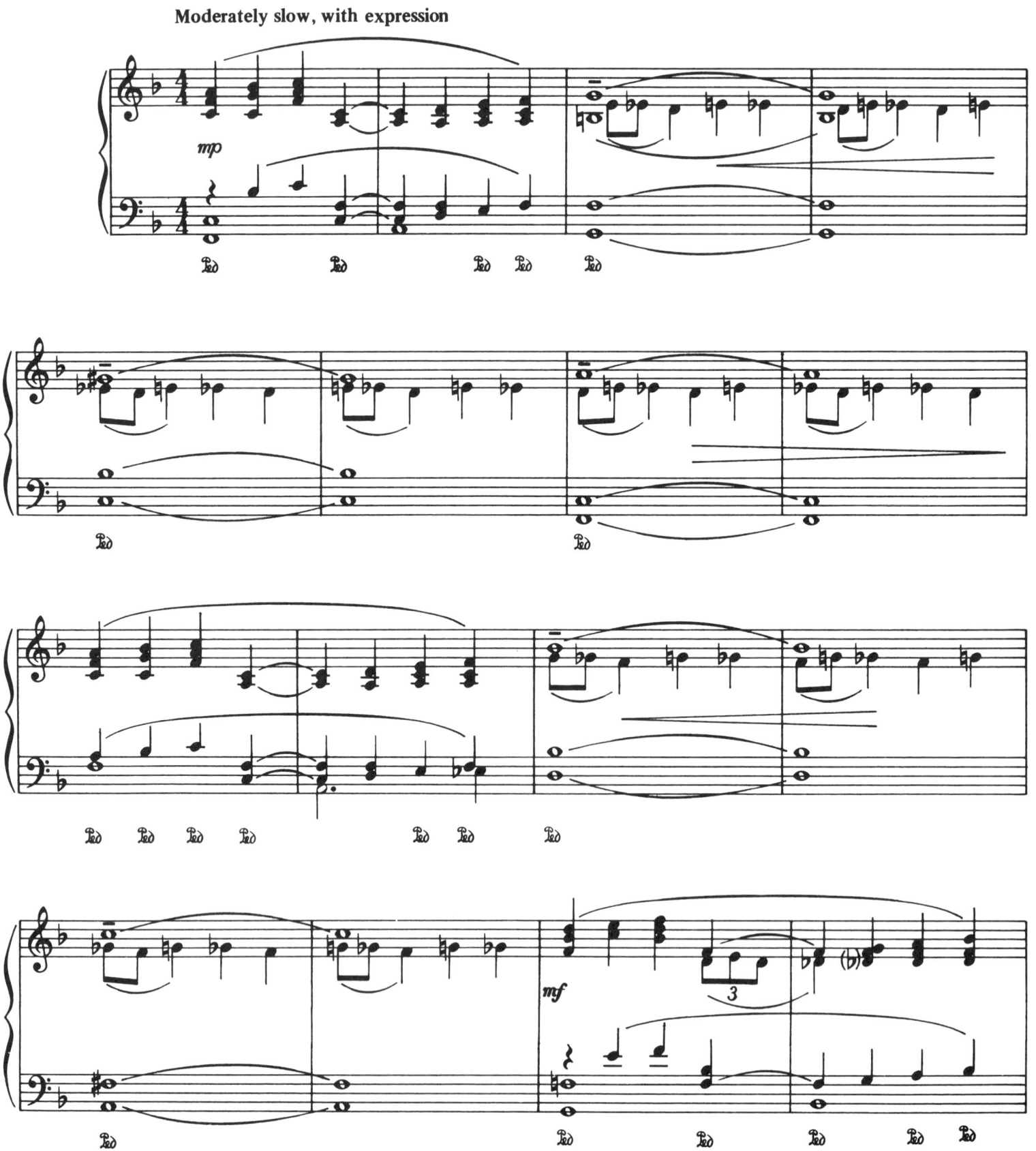

© Copyright 1924 (Renewed) Chappell & Company Incorporated, USA.
This arrangement © Copyright 2000 Chappell & Company Incorporated.
Warner Chappell Music Limited, Griffin House, 161 Hammersmith Road, London W6.
All Rights Reserved. International Copyright Secured.

Nice Work If You Can Get It

Words & Music by George Gershwin & Ira Gershwin

© Copyright 1937 (Renewed) Chappell & Company Incorporated, USA.
This arrangement © Copyright 2000 Chappell & Company Incorporated.
Warner Chappell Music Limited, Griffin House, 161 Hammersmith Road, London W6.
All Rights Reserved. International Copyright Secured.

It Ain't Necessarily So

Words & Music by George Gershwin, Ira Gershwin, DuBose Heyward & Dorothy Heyward

© Copyright 1935 (Renewed) Chappell & Company Incorporated, USA.
This arrangement © Copyright 2000 Chappell & Company Incorporated.
Warner Chappell Music Limited, Griffin House. 161 Hammersmith Road, London W6.
All Rights Reserved. International Copyright Secured.

Summertime

Words & Music by George Gershwin, Ira Gershwin, DuBose Heyward & Dorothy Heyward

© Copyright 1935 (Renewed) Chappell & Company Incorporated, USA.
This arrangement © Copyright 2000 Chappell & Company Incorporated.
Warner Chappell Music Limited, Griffin House, 161 Hammersmith Road, London W6.
All Rights Reserved. International Copyright Secured.

'S Wonderful

Words & Music by George Gershwin & Ira Gershwin

© Copyright 1927 (Renewed) Chappell & Company Incorporated, USA.
This arrangement © Copyright 2000 Chappell & Company Incorporated.
Warner Chappell Music Limited, Griffin House, 161 Hammersmith Road, London W6.
All Rights Reserved. International Copyright Secured.

Embraceable You

Words & Music by George Gershwin & Ira Gershwin

A Foggy Day

Words & Music by George Gershwin & Ira Gershwin

© Copyright 1937 (Renewed) Chappell & Company Incorporated, USA.
This arrangement © Copyright 2000 Chappell & Company Incorporated.
Warner Chappell Music Limited, Griffin House, 161 Hammersmith Road, London W6.
All Rights Reserved. International Copyright Secured.

The Man I Love

Words & Music by George Gershwin & Ira Gershwin

© Copyright 1924 (Renewed) Chappell & Company Incorporated, USA.
This arrangement © Copyright 2000 Chappell & Company Incorporated.
Warner Chappell Music Limited, Griffin House, 161 Hammersmith Road, London W6.
All Rights Reserved. International Copyright Secured.

Strike Up The Band

Words & Music by George Gershwin & Ira Gershwin

They Can't Take That Away From Me

Words & Music by George Gershwin & Ira Gershwin

Somebody Loves Me

Music by George Gershwin

Eb Ab9 Bb11 Bb9 Eb Fm7 Bb7(b9)
Eb Fm7 Bb7 Eb Cm6
Gm Eb9 Am7 D7 Gm Gm7
C9 C7 Fm7 Edim Fm7 Edim Fm7 C7(b9)
Fm7 C7(b9) Fm Cm7 F7(b5) Cm7 F7(b5)

Bb11
E9(b5)
Eb
sfz
sfz
Ped.
Ped.
Amb
Eb
Ab9
Eb
F♯dim
Fm7(b9)
Ab9
Eb
Fm7
8va
loco
Eb6-9
B13
Bb13
Eb
Fm7
Bb7(b9)
Eb
Cb9
Eb
Cm7

Ab9 Bb11 Eb6 Cm Fm7
Eb Cm7 Fm7 Bb7(b9) Eb
Cm6 Gm A13(b9) D9
Gm7 C7 tacet Fm C7
Fm Cm Fm7 Fm (♯7) Fm7 Fm6

F9
loco
8va
Bb+7
Eb
Fm7 (b5)
Bb7(b9)
Eb
Ab9
Gm7(b5)
C9
Fm7
Bb9
Gm7(b5)
C9
Fm7
Bb9
Gm7 (b5)
C9
Fm7
Ema7
Eb6
Ebma7
molto rall.

But Not For Me

Words & Music by George Gershwin & Ira Gershwin

F9
Bb11
Bb13(b9)
Eb9
Eb7
Bbm7
Eb7
G(Ab bass)
Ab
F♯dim
Eb
Cm
G7
Cm
F9(b5)
Fm7
Bb9
B9(b5)
Bb9
tecet
F9
Bb11
Bb13
Eb

F9
Bb11
Bb13(b9)
(b)
Eb7
Eb7
Bbm7
Eb7
G(Abbass)
Ab
F♯dim
Eb
G13
(b)
Cm
C7+
(b)
Fm7
Bb7
1.
Eb
F♯dim
3
Bb7 (sus4)
tacet
2.
Eb
Db9
Eb6-9.

Fascinating Rhythm

Words & Music by George Gershwin & Ira Gershwin

Bb7
Bbm7
Eb13
Bbm7
Eb13
Bbm7
Eb9
Bbm7
Eb13
Bbm7
Eb9
A7(b5)
Ab
Cm7
Fm7
Bb7
Bb9+
Eb
Eb6-9
Cm
Cm7
Am7(b5)
F13
F13(b9)
Bb7
Gdim
Bb7
C♯dim
Fm7
Bb13
Fm7
Bb13

Fm7 Bb13 Fm7 Bb7 Bbm7 Eb13
Bbm7 Eb13 Bbm7 Eb9 Bbm7 Eb13 Eb9 A7(b5)
Ab Fm7 Dm7(b5) G7 Cm Ebma 7 F7
Fm7 Bb13 Fm7 F9 Bb13 Eb F♯dim
1.
Fm7 Bb9 Edim Eb tacet Eb6
2.
sfz

Oh, Lady, Be Good

Words & Music by George Gershwin & Ira Gershwin

F Gb13 Gm7 C13 (b5-b9) F
sfz sfz
Bb9 F D7(b9)
3 3 3
Gm7 C7 Gm7 C7
3 3 3 3
F6 C7 F F7 Bb
3
Bdim F C7 F
3

G13
G7
Gm7
C13
Gm7
Gb9
F
Bb9
F
Gm7
F
Gm7
F
Abdim
Gm7
C7
Gm7
C13
F
Db9
Gm7
C13
F6
Bb9
F

F♯dim
Gm7
C13
F6
Db9
Gm7
Gb7(9+)
F
Bb9
F
Am7
G♯dim
Gm7
Gb7
Fma7
Cm7
F7(b5)
Bb
Bdim

51

An American In Paris

By George Gershwin

Allegretto grazioso

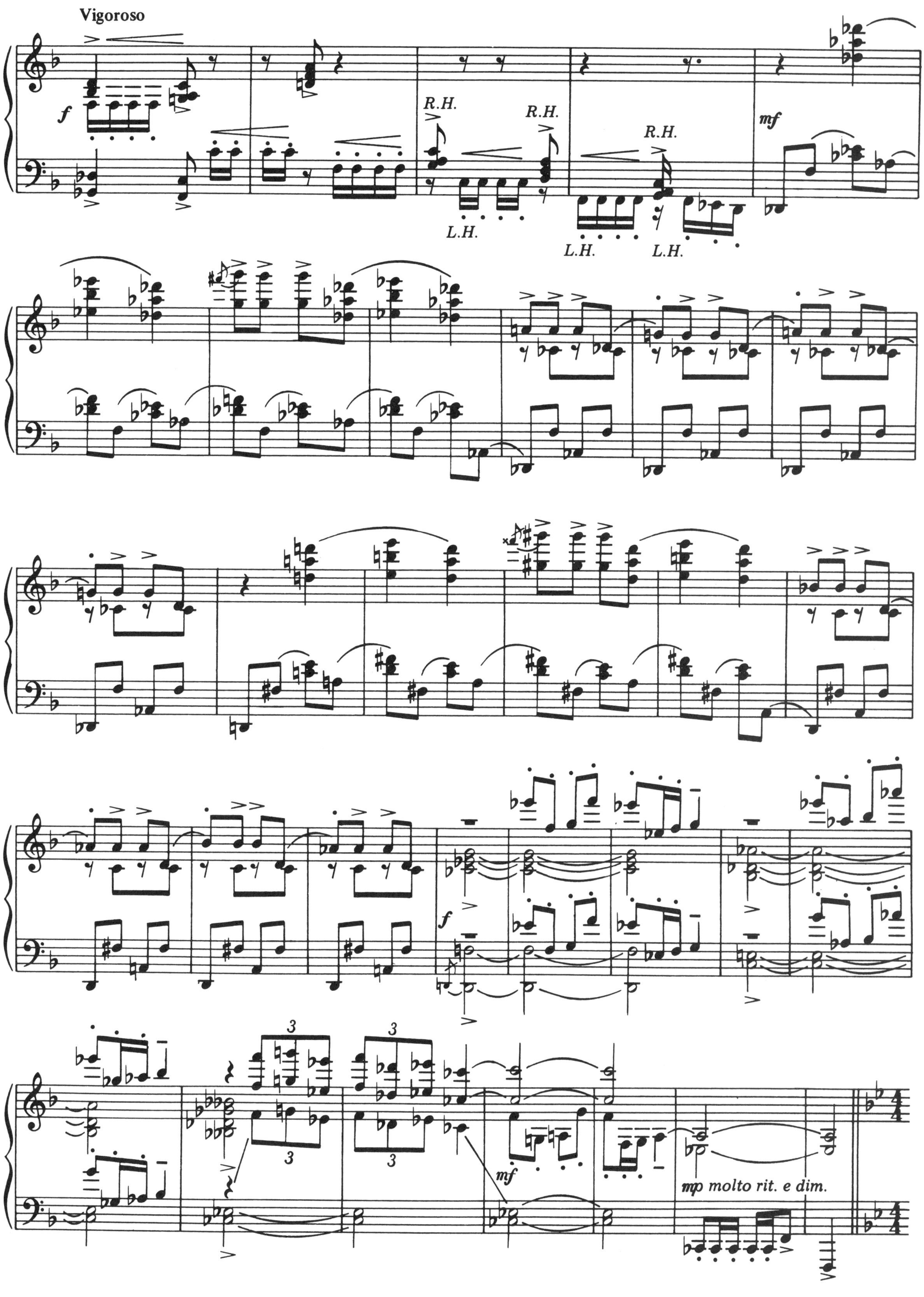
Vigoroso
f
R.H.
R.H.
L.H.
R.H.
L.H.
L.H.
mf
f
3
3
3
3
mf
mp molto rit. e dim.

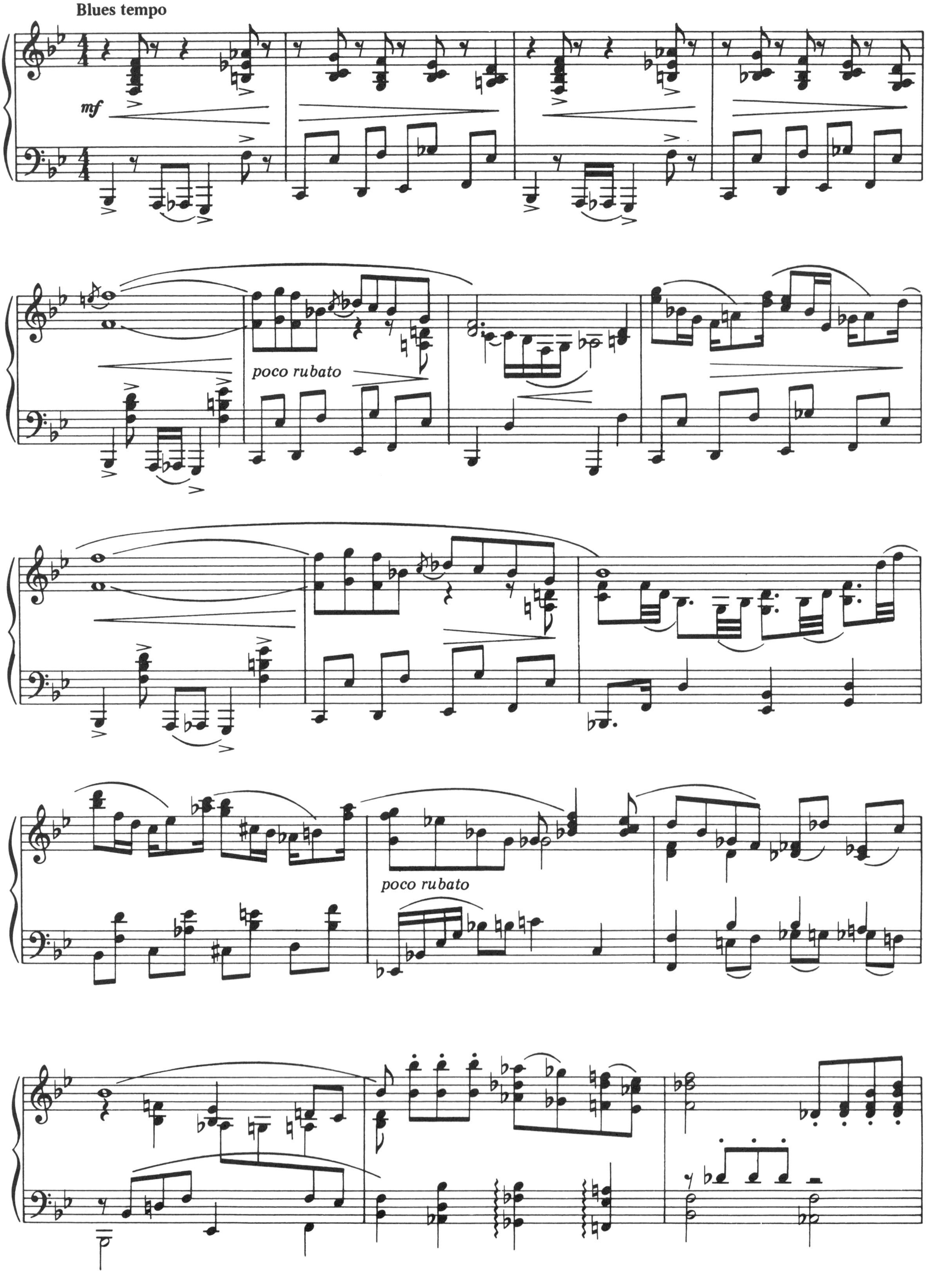
Blues tempo
mf
poco rubato
poco rubato

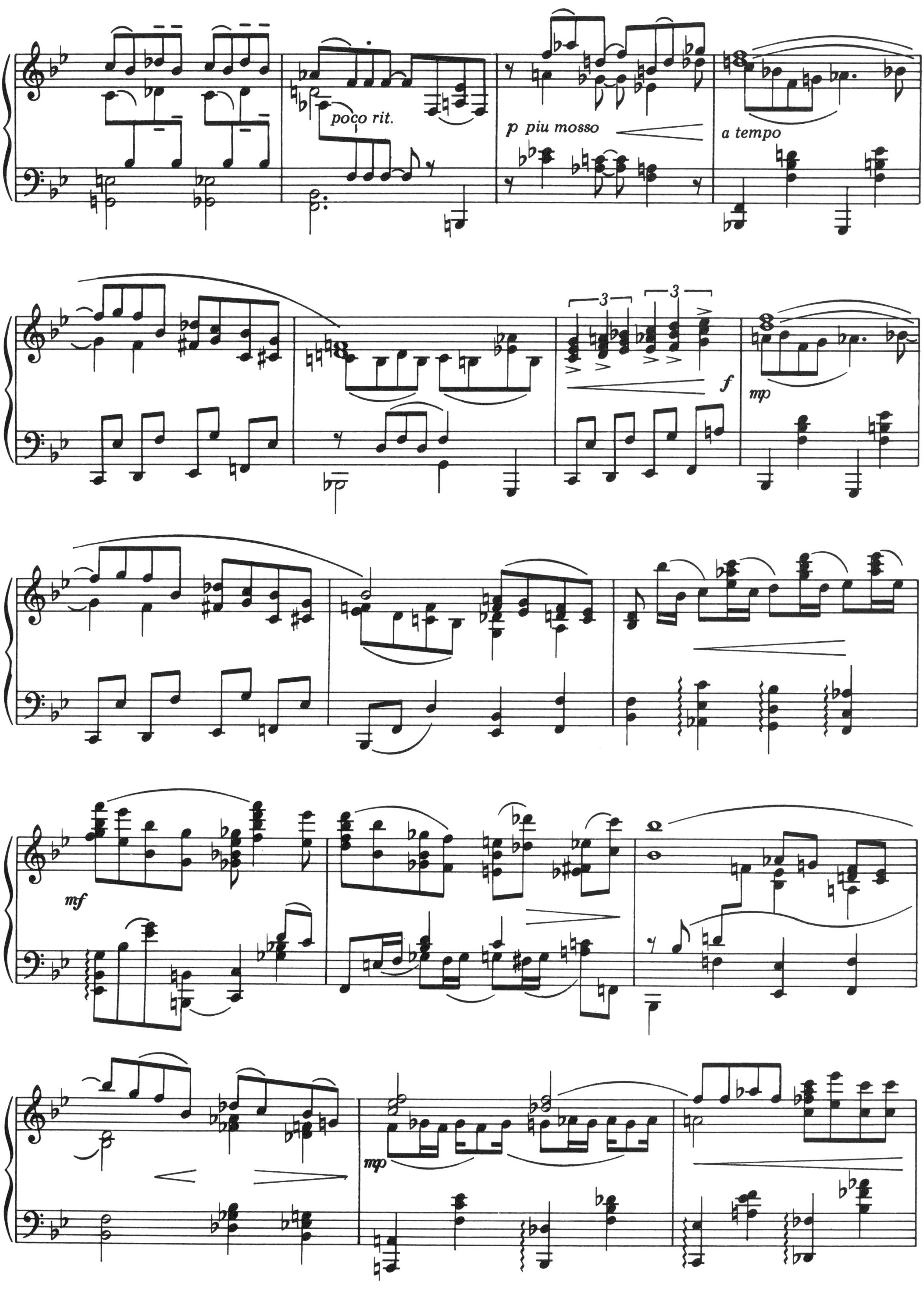
poco rit.
p piu mosso
a tempo
3
3
f
mp
mf
mp
mp

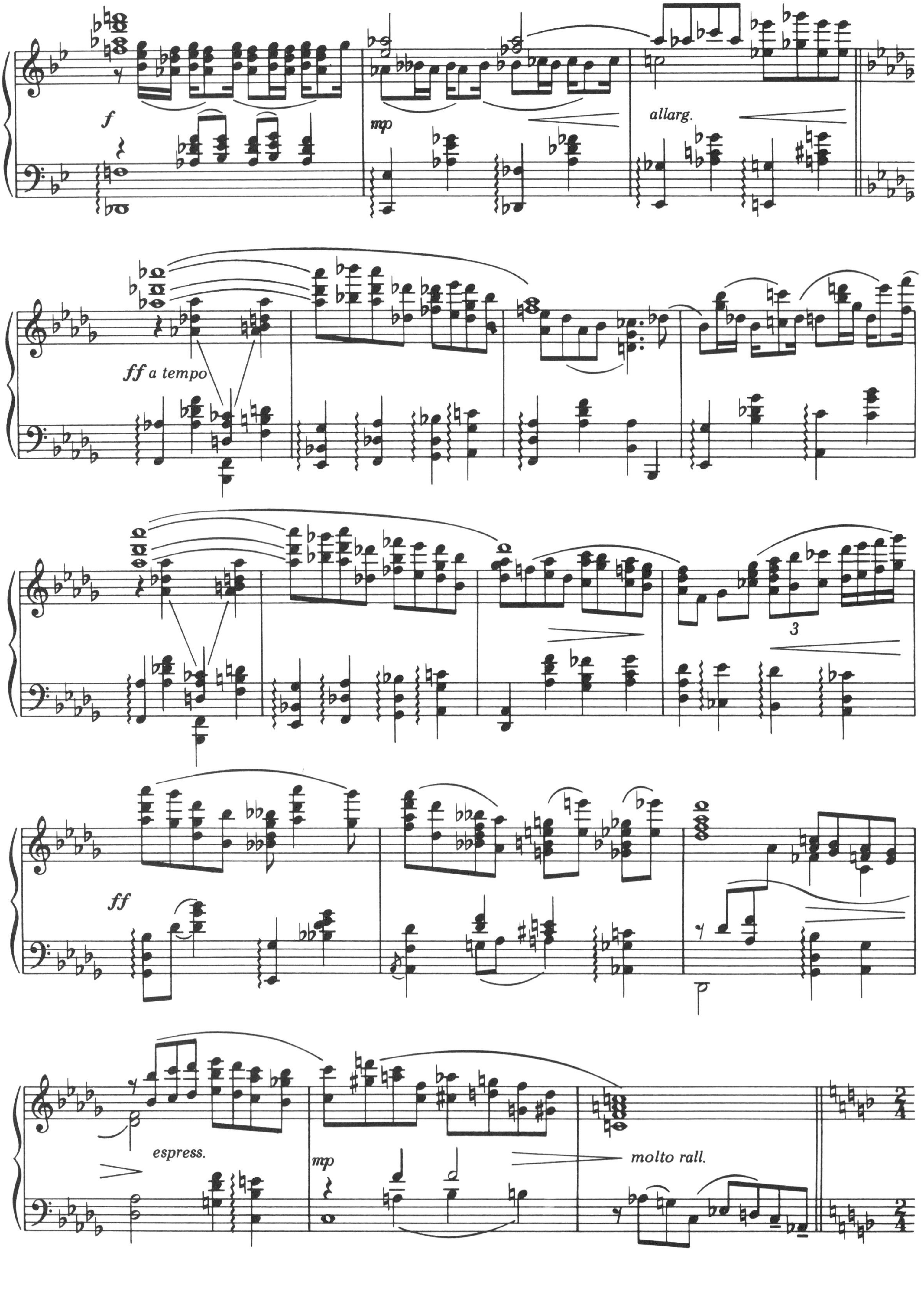
f
mp
allarg.
ff a tempo
3
ff
espress.
mp
molto rall.

Allegretto grazioso
p
Vigoroso
f
L.H.
rit.
Allegro
mf con anima

58

59

I Got Rhythm

Words & Music by George Gershwin & Ira Gershwin

Bb
C♯dim
Cm7
F13 (b5-b9)
Dm7
C♯dim
Gm7
F7(b5)
Bb
Bb7
Eb
Ebm
Bb
F7
Bb
D9
Am7
D9
Am7
G7
C9
Gm7
C9
Gm7
F7
Cm7

G♯dim F7 Bb C♯dim Cm7 F7(b5-b9) Dm7 C♯dim
Cm7 B9(b5) Bb Bb7 Eb Gb7
Bb Fm E7 G7+ C9 F7
Bb tacet Bb Gdim Cm7 F13 (b9)
Dm7 C♯dim Gm7 F7 Bb Bb7

Eb Ebm B7 F7 Bb Db9 Cm7 Cb9(b5)
Bb C♯dim Cm7 F13(b9) Dm7 C♯dim
Cm7 F7 Bb Bb7 Eb Ebm
Bb F7 B6 D9(b5)
G7

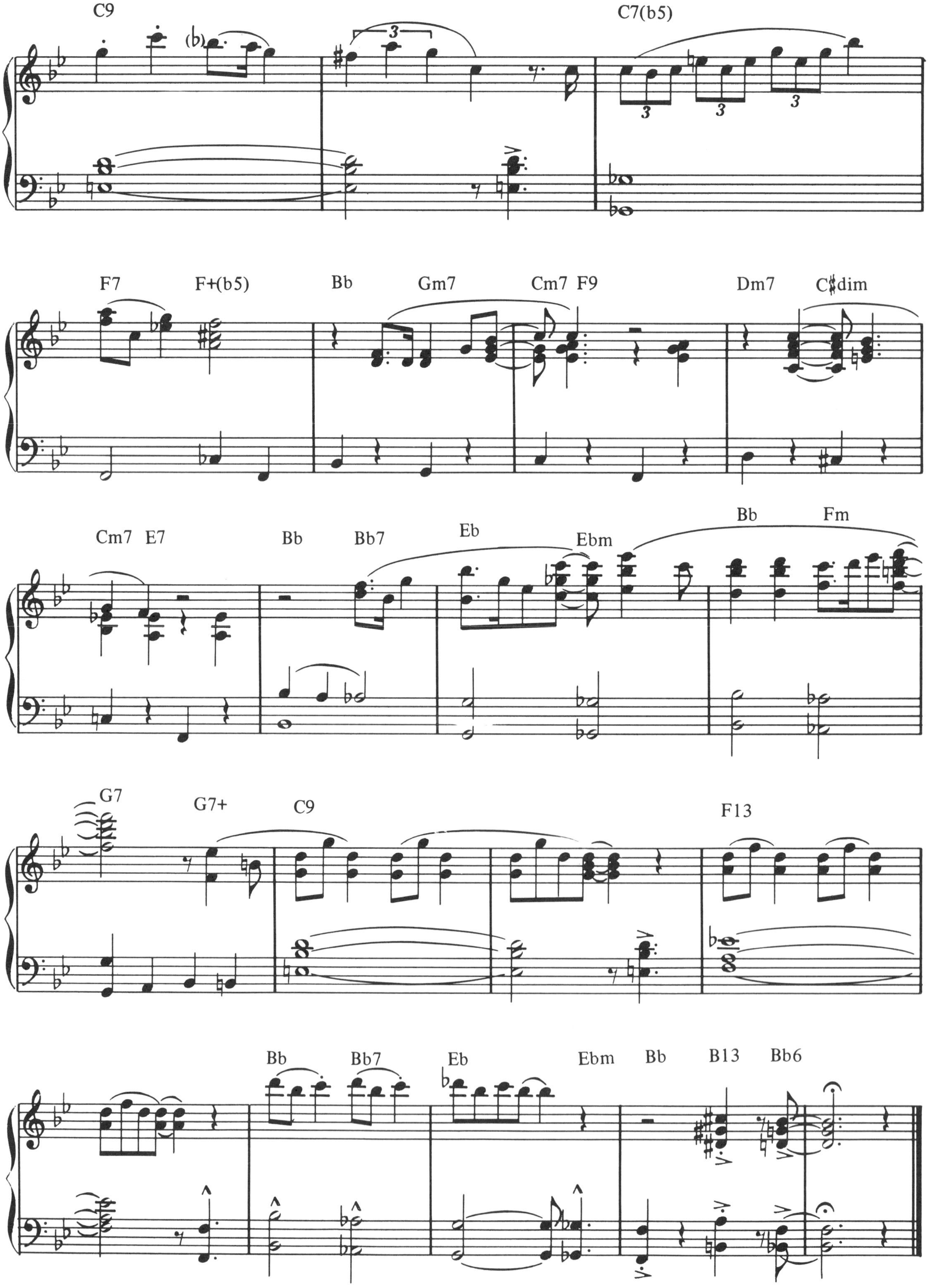

Printed in Malta by Interprint Limited
4/01 (40131)